BUTTERFIELD SCHOOL
1441 LAKE STREET
LIBERTYVILLE, IL 60048

DEMCO

HOCKEY
MIRACLE ON ICE

by Michael Sandler

Consultant: Jim Bugenhagen
Director of Hockey, Sky Rink
Chelsea Piers
New York, New York

BEARPORT
PUBLISHING COMPANY, INC.

New York, New York

Credits

Editorial development by Judy Nayer

Cover and title page, Heinz Kluetmeier/Sports Illustrated; 4-5, AP/Wide World Photos; 5 (inset), Bruce Bennett Studios/Getty Images; 6, Joe Le Monnier; 7, OmniPhoto Communications, Inc.; 8, Kenneth Batelman; 9, Focus on Sport/Getty Images; 10-11, ©Wally McNamee/CORBIS; 11 (inset), Peter Read Miller/Sports Illustrated; 12, STAFF/AFP/Getty Images; 13, STAFF/AFP/Getty Images; 14-15 (both), Bruce Bennett Studios/Getty Images; 16, Douglas Ball/AP/Wide World Photos; 17, AP/Wide World Photos; 18-19, Focus on Sport/Getty Images; 20, Jerry Cooke/Sports Illustrated; 21, George Tiedemann/Sports Illustrated; 22, Bill Eppridge/Sports Illustrated; 23, AP/Wide World Photos; 24, Getty Images; 25, Heinz Kluetmeier/Sports Illustrated; 26, Bruce Bennett Studios/Getty Images; 27, Keystone/CNP/Getty Images; 29, David E. Klutho/Sports Illustrated.

Design and production by
Ralph Cosentino

Library of Congress Cataloging-in-Publication Data

Sandler, Michael.
  Hockey : miracle on ice / by Michael Sandler.
     p. cm. — (Upsets & comebacks)
  Includes bibliographical references and index.
  ISBN 1-59716-168-3 (library binding) — ISBN 1-59716-194-2 (pbk.)
  1. Hockey—United States—Juvenile literature. 2. Hockey teams—United States—Juvenile literature. 3. Winter Olympic Games (13th : 1980 : Lake Placid, N.Y.)—Juvenile literature. I. Title. II. Series.

  GV847.25.S26 2006
  796.9620973—dc22

                              2005026085

For more information, write to Bearport Publishing Company, Inc., 101 Fifth Avenue, Suite 6R, New York, New York 10003. Printed in the United States of America.

1 2 3 4 5 6 7 8 9 10

Table of Contents

Ready for the Face-Off

The young players of the 1980 U.S. Olympic hockey team were ready for the **face-off**. They were ready to begin play. They were ready for the biggest challenge of their lives.

If the U.S. team won, they were **guaranteed** an Olympic medal. Standing in their way, however, stood the best hockey team in the world—the Soviets.

The 1980 U.S. ice hockey team

Ten thousand fans were waiting in the stands. Few people believed the Americans stood a chance of winning. One person who did was the U.S. coach, Herb Brooks. He told each team member: "You were born to be a player. You were meant to be here. This moment is yours."

U.S. Olympic hockey team coach Herb Brooks

In 1980, the United States had the youngest Olympic hockey team in history. Most of the players were in their early 20s. One, Mike Ramsey, was just 19 years old.

The Game of Ice Hockey

Hockey is a cold-weather, winter sport. It is played on ice by two **opposing** teams. Players wear skates to speed across the slick frozen surface. They carry curved wooden sticks while skating.

Players use their sticks to control the puck, a hard, flat rubber disk. They can use their sticks to catch, tap, pass, and slap the puck across the ice.

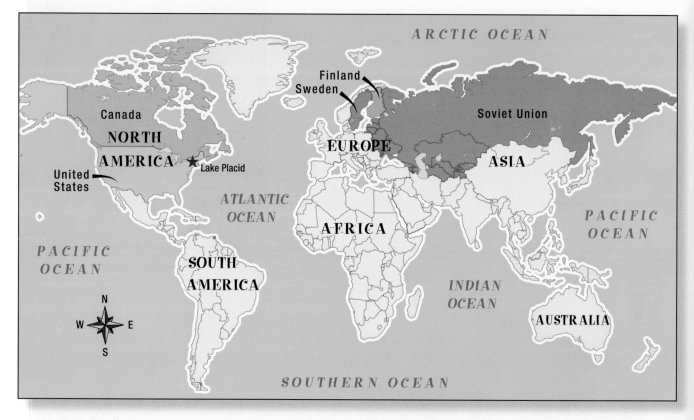

This map shows the Soviet Union in 1980. The Soviet Union no longer exists today. In 1991, it broke up into many separate countries, with Russia being the largest.

The team with the puck tries to score a goal by shooting it into a net. The other team tries to stop them and get the puck back. The team with the most goals at the end of the game wins.

These boys play ice hockey on a frozen pond.

Ice hockey began in Canada in the 1800s. Stick-and-ball games usually played on grassy fields were adapted for playing on frozen ponds in winter.

Playing the Game

Ice hockey has **official** rules. Each team has six players on the ice at a time. A game is divided into three 20-minute periods.

Forwards work together to score goals for their team.

Defensemen skate near the net. They help the goalie keep the other team from scoring.

There are goals, or "nets," at each end of the rink.

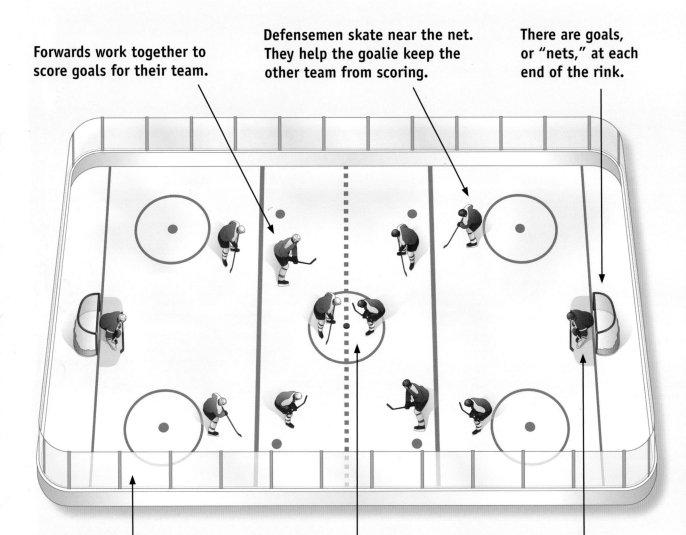

Wooden and plastic walls with tall glass keep the puck and players from flying out of the rink.

Play begins in a "face-off" circle. A referee drops the puck between two players. Each tries to gain control of the puck with his stick.

Goaltenders, or goalies, use their sticks, gloves, and bodies to stop the other team's shots. Stopping a shot is called "making a save."

On the rink, the action can be rough. Hockey players often check, or slam, their bodies into one another. The action is also fast. Hockey players move faster than players in any other team sport. The puck moves fast, too. A **slap shot** can whip across the rink at over 100 miles per hour (161 kph). To safeguard themselves from body checks, swinging sticks, and dangerous flying pucks, hockey players wear protective **gear**.

A hockey team's 20 players take turns playing and resting. Only five players and one goalie are on the ice at a time.

The Winter Olympics

Every four years, sports teams from different nations come together to join in the Olympic Games. At the Winter Olympics, thousands of athletes **compete** in cold-weather sports such as figure skating, snowboarding, and skiing. Ice hockey is one of the most popular events.

Opening Ceremony at the 1980 Winter Olympics

The Winter Olympics move from country to country. In 1980, they were held in the United States. The site was Lake Placid, New York. American sports fans were thrilled by the chance to see the games in person. The U.S. hockey team was guaranteed to have plenty of fans rooting for it.

Snowboarding became an Olympic sport in 1998. Here Kelly Clark, from the United States, does a halfpipe at the 2002 Winter Olympics.

At the Olympics, the team or athlete who wins an event gets a gold medal. A silver medal is awarded for second place. A bronze medal is given for third place.

The Kings of Olympic Hockey

People looked forward to watching the Americans. They expected, however, that the Soviet Union would win the **tournament**.

The Soviets were the kings of Olympic hockey. They had the toughest, most highly skilled hockey players in the world. They had played together for years.

The Soviets had full control over the puck. They made dazzling passes. They played the game as well as it could be played.

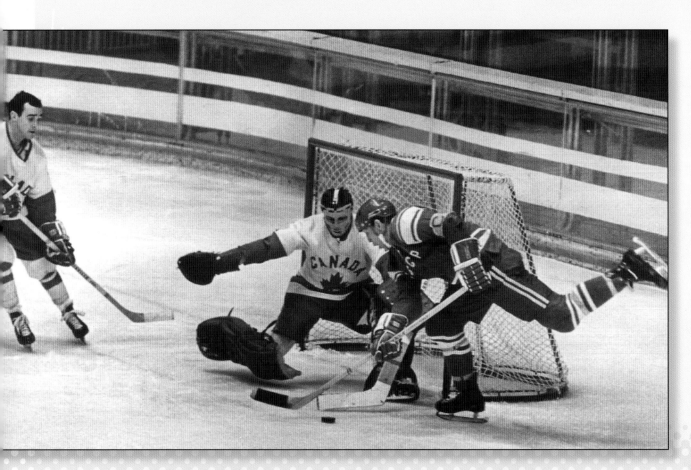

Soviet hockey player Anatoly Firsov tries to fire a shot past the Canadian goalie during the 1968 Winter Olympics.

They had won 27 out of their last 28 Olympic games. They had left the last four Winter Olympics wearing gold medals. Any country that wanted the gold would have to beat the Soviets.

The Soviet hockey team celebrates after beating the Canadian hockey team during the 1968 Winter Olympics.

From 1954-1991, the Soviets were considered the best **amateur** hockey team in the world.

The U.S. Team

The U.S. hockey team was very different from the Soviet team. The players hadn't won any Olympic medals. They hadn't played together for many years.

These athletes had been thrown together the summer before the Olympics. They were young men from college and minor league teams around the country.

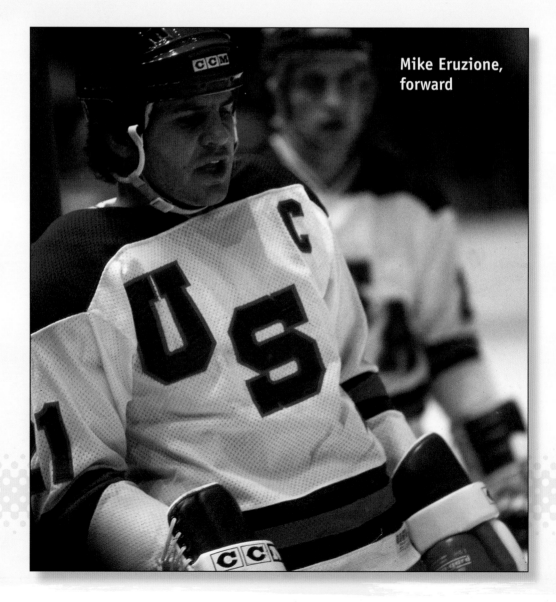

Mike Eruzione, forward

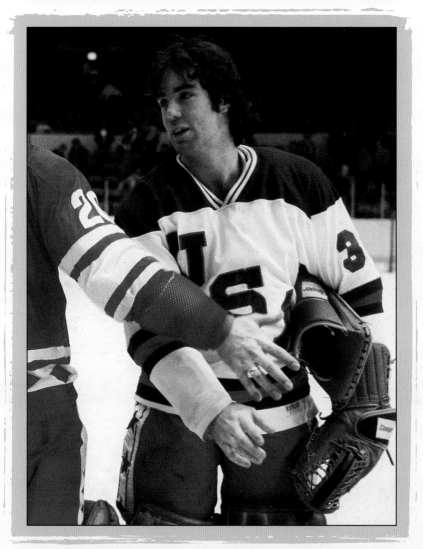

Jim Craig, goaltender

Most players came from states like Minnesota, Wisconsin, Michigan, and Massachusetts. In these places, winters were cold and hockey was a popular sport.

For most of these players, just making the team was a dream come true. Some dreamed of winning a medal. Not many, however, seriously thought about beating the Soviets.

> Over 400 hockey players tried out for the 1980 American team. Only 20 players made it.

Coach Herb Brooks, however, was serious about beating the Soviets. They were very skilled players. To help improve his players' skills, he came up with a special style of hockey.

He taught his players to never give up the puck. "Don't just dump it down the ice toward the goal," he told them. "Move it around. Pass it. Work together."

Coach Brooks speaks to members of the 1980 U.S. hockey team during a practice.

The Soviets also had more experience than the Americans. So, Coach Brooks took his team on **grueling** road trips. The players went from town to town. They traveled to foreign countries. They played against college, **pro**, and **international** teams. Game by game, they grew stronger.

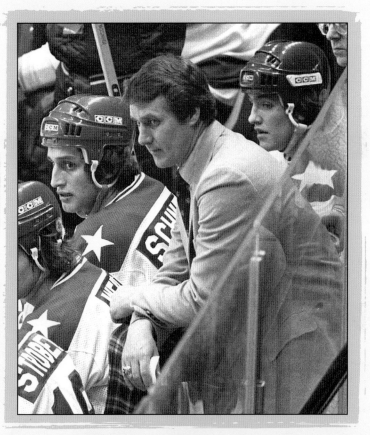

Coach Brooks watches his team.

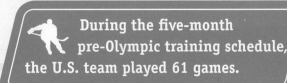
During the five-month pre-Olympic training schedule, the U.S. team played 61 games.

17

Opening Round

Finally, the 1980 Olympics began. In the first game, the United States faced Sweden. The Swedes were tough. With less than a minute left, the Americans were behind by a goal. If they lost, any chance of winning a medal would probably be lost as well.

The U.S. hockey team celebrates after scoring against the Swedes.

The clock ticked down. The game was slipping away. Suddenly, the puck flew near defenseman Bill Baker. Bill swung his stick. Goal!

The crowd was thrilled. The game ended in a tie that kept U.S. medal hopes alive. Then the United States won its next four games. The young Americans were headed to the medal round!

Red Group	wins	losses	ties
Soviet Union	5	0	0
Finland	3	2	0
Canada	3	2	0
Poland	2	3	0
Holland	1	3	1
Blue Group	wins	losses	ties
Sweden	4	0	1
United States	4	0	1
Czechoslovakia	3	2	0
Romania	1	3	1
West Germany	1	4	0

The highlighted teams were the ones that would move on to the medal round.

Olympic ice hockey has two rounds. In the opening round, the teams are split into red and blue groups. The two teams in each group that win the most games go to the medal round.

The Soviets

Next up was a game against the powerful Soviets. The streets of Lake Placid were buzzing. All people could talk about was hockey. *The Americans are doing great, but can they really beat the Soviet Union?* asked the fans.

Eager fans brave the cold to buy tickets to the Olympic games.

The Soviets were confident. They had **trounced** the U.S. team 10–3 in a practice game a few weeks earlier.

"What can change in two weeks?" asked one Soviet player.

Surprisingly, the Americans were confident. They felt they were a better team than before. They had proven it in their last five games.

"We're going to do it," predicted U.S. goaltender Jim Craig.

After the opening round, the red team winner plays the second-place blue team. The blue team winner then plays the second-place red team. The winners of those games then play for the gold medal.

Finally the game began. The Soviets quickly showed what made them great. They charged toward the American goal. They **launched** shot after shot. Jim Craig made several difficult saves, but one slid through. The Soviets had the lead.

Jim Craig makes a save.

This goal, shot by Mike Eruzione (not shown), won the game for the U.S. team.

Minutes later, the **arena** erupted in cheers when the United States tied the game. Then the Soviets scored again. Then the Americans. It was 2–2, then 3–3. Who would win? Fans were going crazy.

The Americans sent the puck past the Soviet defenders. Mike Eruzione caught it and smacked it straight into the Soviets' net! It was the game's final goal. The United States had won!

In the medal round game, the Soviets took 23 more shots at the goal than the Americans did. Goalie Jim Craig stopped all but three of them.

Going for the Gold

After beating the Soviet Union, the United States was guaranteed a silver medal. They weren't interested in silver, however. Now they wanted only one thing—the gold medal.

Two days later, the United States took to the ice against Finland in the championship game. Once again, the U.S. team fell behind. Once again, they fought back and **surged** into the lead. When the final buzzer sounded, the Americans had a 4–2 victory. It was nothing less than a miracle.

The players had **overcome** their youth. They had overcome the most powerful hockey teams in the world. The U.S. team had won the Olympic gold!

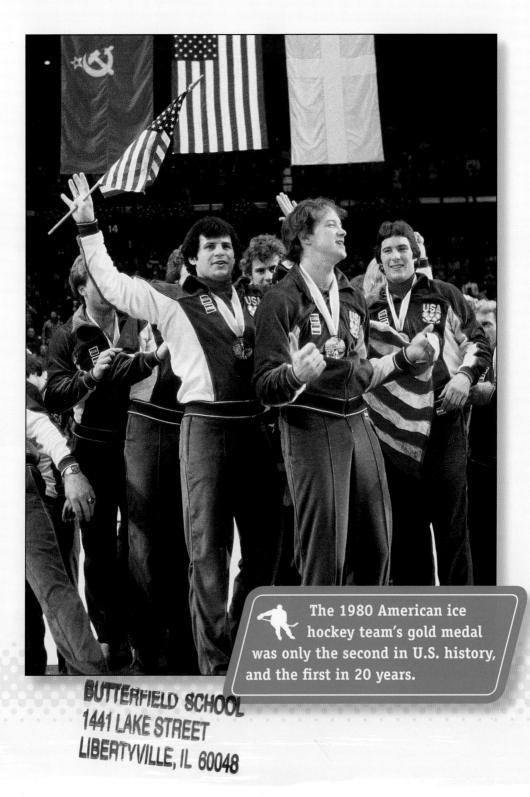

The 1980 American ice hockey team's gold medal was only the second in U.S. history, and the first in 20 years.

BUTTERFIELD SCHOOL
1441 LAKE STREET
LIBERTYVILLE, IL 60048

After the Miracle

Coach Brooks had done the impossible. He took a group of young, inexperienced players and, in just six months, turned them into the world's finest hockey team.

All over the country, people celebrated the team's achievement. This hockey team had made an entire country proud.

Some of the players went on to success in pro hockey. Others moved out of the spotlight. All of them, however, will always be remembered for what they **accomplished** at the 1980 Olympics. They will be remembered for what they proved: *If you work hard and believe in yourself, there are no limits to success.*

After their victory, the U.S. Olympic team was invited to the White House to meet President Jimmy Carter.

Coach Herb Brooks died in 2003. Twenty-five hundred people attended his funeral, including many former players from the team.

Just the Facts

More About Skating, Ice Hockey, and the Olympics

★ **Ancient Skates**—Hockey is a fairly new sport. However, ice skating dates back thousands of years. Long ago, people in northern Europe used ice skates when hunting animals on frozen, icy terrain. Their blades were made of bone and were attached to boots with leather straps.

★ **Super Soviets**—The Soviet team bounced back at the 1980 Olympics to beat Sweden for the bronze medal. They didn't lose another international game for five more years.

★ **Making the Cut**—Choosing players for the U.S. Olympic ice hockey team couldn't have been easy for Coach Brooks. He knew firsthand how it felt to be left out. In 1960, he was the last man left off of the U.S. Olympic ice hockey team. The team went on to win the gold—without him.

★ **Puck-cakes**—Hockey pucks are made just like cupcakes. They're baked. First, rubber is mixed with other ingredients. The mix is rolled into logs, and then sliced into disks. The disks are placed in molds like cupcake pans. They are baked for about 20 minutes. Then they are ready to use.

★ **Going Pro**—Several members of the U.S. Olympic team went on to play in the National Hockey League, known as the NHL. The league is composed of pro teams in Canada and the United States.

The Gear

All hockey players need special gear. Goaltenders, however, wear the most—50 pounds (23 kg) of equipment.

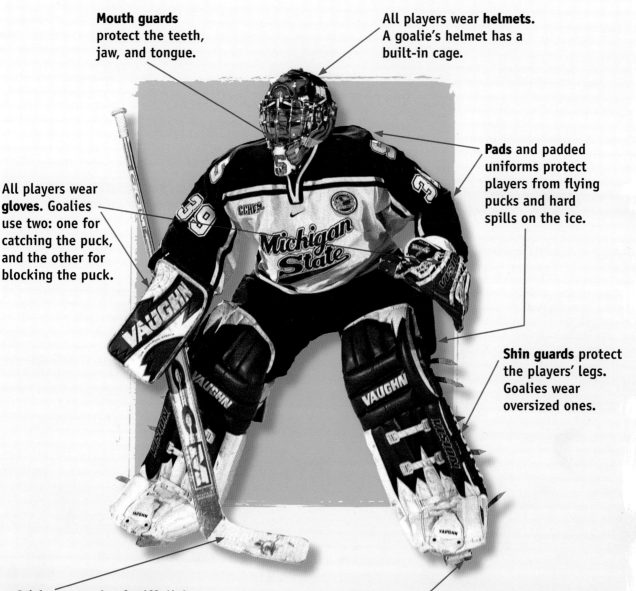

Mouth guards protect the teeth, jaw, and tongue.

All players wear **helmets**. A goalie's helmet has a built-in cage.

All players wear **gloves**. Goalies use two: one for catching the puck, and the other for blocking the puck.

Pads and padded uniforms protect players from flying pucks and hard spills on the ice.

Shin guards protect the players' legs. Goalies wear oversized ones.

Sticks are made of stiff, light material such as aluminum, fiberglass, or graphite.

Hockey skates have grooved stainless steel blades that dig into the ice to provide speed and control. The bulletproof material around the foot protects players' feet from the blades of other skaters.

Glossary

accomplished (uh-KOM-plishd) succeeded in doing

amateur (AM-uh-chur) athletes who don't receive money for playing a sport

arena (uh-REE-nuh) a large building where sporting events are held

compete (kuhm-PEET) play as hard as possible in order to win

face-off (FAYSS-awf) when two players from opposing teams start play by battling for a puck dropped on the ice by a referee

gear (GIHR) equipment or clothing designed for a special purpose

grueling (GROO-uh-ling) very hard, difficult, or tiring

guaranteed (ga-ruhn-TEED) promised

international (*in*-tur-NASH-uh-nuhl) from countries around the world

launched (LAWNCHT) sent into motion

official (uh-FISH-ul) approved by the people who are in charge

opposing (uh-POZE-ing) against; opposing teams are teams that are playing against each other

overcome (*oh*-vur-KUHM) successfully handle a problem or challenge

pro (PROH) short for "professional," a player who gets paid to play sports

slap shot (SLAP SHOT) a powerful hockey shot made by first raising the stick high and then slapping the puck

surged (SURJD) moved forward quickly

tournament (TUR-nuh-muhnt) a series of games or contests that result in one player or team being chosen as champion

trounced (TROUNST) defeated by a huge amount

Bibliography

Carroll, M. R. *The Concise Encyclopedia of Hockey*. Vancouver, Canada: Greystone Books (2001).

Coffey, Wayne. *The Boys of Winter: The Untold Story of a Coach, a Dream, and the 1980 U.S. Olympic Hockey Team*. New York: Crown (2005).

Thomas, Keltie. *How Hockey Works*. Toronto, Canada: Maple Tree Press (2002).

Wallechinsky, David. *The Complete Book of the Winter Olympics*. New York: Overlook Press (2001).

Wendel, Tim. *Going for the Gold*. Westport, CT: Lawrence Hill & Co. (1981).

Read More

Ditchfield, Christin. *Ice Hockey*. Danbury, CT: Children's Press (2003).

Kennedy, Mike. *Ice Hockey*. Danbury, CT: Franklin Watts (2003).

Macy, Sue. *Freeze Frame: A Photographic History of the Winter Olympics*. New York: National Geographic Children's Books (2006).

Will, Sandra. *Hockey for Fun!* Minneapolis, MN: Compass Point Books (2003).

Learn More Online

Visit these Web sites to learn more about ice hockey and the Winter Olympics:

www.collectionscanada.ca/hockey/kids/index-e.html

www.exploratorium.edu/hockey/

www.nhl.com/kids/

www.usolympicteam.com/kids/

Index

About the Author

Michael Sandler lives in Brooklyn, New York. He has written
numerous books on sports for children and young adults.
His two children, Laszlo and Asha, are not quite old enough
to read them yet.